The Beaver Scout S

Compiled by Tracey H
Designed by Colin Phillips
Illustrations by Ron Branagan

Acknowledgements

Thanks to all Leaders and Commissioners in the Beaver Scout Section who have contributed to the selection of songs included in this Song Book.

'Hey Little Beaver' (Copyright Control) words and music by
Malcolm A. Lycett

'It's a small, small world' (Campbell Connelly and Co. Ltd.) words and music by
Sherman and Sherman

Copyright 1995
The Scout Association
Baden-Powell House, Queen's Gate, London SW7 5JS

First Edition
ISBN 0 85165 291 3
Reprinted 1995

Contents: Page No.

Alice the camel	3
A great big Beaver smile	4
BINGO	5
Brush your teeth	6
Baby bumble bee	7
Cecil is a caterpillar	8
Everywhere we go	9
Little green frog	10
Goodnight Beavers	11
The grand old Duke of York	12
Frog song	13
Hey little Beaver	14
I'm a little beaver	15
If you're a Beaver and you know it	16
It's a small, small world	17
Land of the silver birch	18
One, two, three little Beavers	19
Pizza Hut	20
Ten brown beavers	21
The beaver swam over the river	22
The wee wee song	23
Chocolate eclairs	24
We are the red men	25
The worm song	26
Camp fire's burning	27
We're all together again	27
Ging gang gooli	28
God's love is like a circle	29
I know a song that'll get on your nerves	30
Kum by yah	31
Old MacDonald	32
Do your ears hang low?	33

Alice the camel

Alice the camel had three humps,
Alice the camel had three humps,
Alice the camel had three humps,
So, go, Alice GO! Bum, bum, bum.

Alice the camel had two humps,
Alice the camel had two humps,
Alice the camel had two humps,
So, go, Alice GO! Bum, bum, bum.

Alice the camel had one hump,
Alice the camel had one hump,
Alice the camel had one hump,
So, go, Alice GO! Bum, bum, bum.

Alice the camel had no humps,
Alice the camel had no humps,
Alice the camel had no humps,
So Alice was a mule!

ACTIONS
When the word 'humps' is sung, the Beaver Scouts bend their knees. When the phrase 'Bum bum bum' is sung, the Beaver Scouts wiggle their bottoms from side to side.

A great big Beaver smile

I've something in my pocket that belongs across my face,
I keep it close beside me in a most convenient place,
You'll never ever guess it, though you'd try for quite a while,
So I'll take it out and put it on, it's a great big Beaver smile!

ACTIONS
The Beaver Scouts mime the words as they are sung, for example, putting a hand into a pocket, drawing a hand across a face and so on.

BINGO

There was a Beaver had a kit,
And Bingo was his name,
B-I-NGO, B-I-NGO, B-I-NGO,
Bingo was his name.

Brush your teeth

Brush, brush, brush your teeth,
Morning noon and night,
See your dentist twice a year,
And you will be alright.

Baby bumble bee

I'm taking home a baby bumble bee,
Won't my mummy be surprised at me,
I'm taking home a baby bumble bee,
Ow! Ow! It stung me!

So I'm squashing up a baby bumble bee,
Won't my mummy be surprised at me,
I'm squashing up a baby bumble bee,
Errr! There's blood on me!

So, I'm licking up a baby bumble bee,
Won't my mummy be surprised at me,
I'm licking up a baby bumble bee,
But errr! There's no salt!

So I'm bringing up a baby bumble bee,
Won't my mummy be surprised at me,
I'm bringing up a baby bumble bee,
But errr! All over me!

I'm washing off the baby bumble bee,
Won't my mummy be surprised at me,
I'm washing of a baby bumble bee,
Hey Mum! What's for tea?

ACTIONS

1st verse: Cup hands to 'take home the bumble bee'.
2nd verse: Squash hands together.
3rd verse: Lick hands.
4th verse: Cup hands.
5th verse: Pretend to wash hands.

Cecil is a caterpillar

Cecil is a caterpillar, Cecil is my friend,
Last time I saw Cecil he was this big ...
I said to Cecil, 'What have you done?'
He said, *'I've eaten my Mum.'*

Cecil is a caterpillar, Cecil is my friend,
Last time I saw Cecil he was this big ...
I said to Cecil, 'What have you done?'
He said, *'I've eaten my Dad!'*

Cecil is a caterpillar, Cecil is my friend,
Last time I saw Cecil he was this big ...
I said to Cecil, 'What have you done?'
He said, *'I've eaten my Grandma and Grandad!'*

Cecil is a caterpillar, Cecil is my friend,
Last time I saw Cecil he was this big ...
I said to Cecil, 'What have you done?'
He said, *'I've been sick!'*

ACTIONS
Beaver Scouts chant lines in *italics*.

Everywhere we go

Everywhere we go,
Everywhere we go,
People always ask us,
People always ask us,
Who we are,
Who we are,
So we tell them,
So we tell them,
We're the (insert Colony name) Beavers,
We're the (insert Colony name) Beavers,
Mighty, mighty Beavers,
Mighty, mighty Beavers,
And if they can't hear us,
And if they can't hear us,
We sing a little louder!
We sing a little louder!

Little green frog

Eyes, tongue went the little green frog one day,
Eyes, tongue went the little green frog one day,
Eyes, tongue went the little green frog one day,
And they all went *Eyes, tongue, (clap)*.

Now we all know frogs go 'Na na na na na
na na na na na, na na na na na.'
They don't go *Eyes, tongue, (clap)*.

Goodnight Beavers

Goodnight Beavers, Goodnight Beavers,
Goodnight Beavers, we're going to go on home.

Merrily we swim on home, swim on home, swim on home,
Merrily we swim on home, down the Beaver pond.

Sweet dreams Beavers, sweet dreams Beavers,
Sweet dreams Beavers, we're going to leave you now.

Merrily we swim on home, swim on home, swim on home,
Merrily we swim on home, down the Beaver pond.

The grand old Duke of York

The grand old Duke of York,
He had ten thousand men,
He marched them up to the top of the hill,
And he marched them down again.

And when they were up they were up,
And when they were down they were down,
And when they were only half way up,
They were neither up nor down.

Frog song

Five little freckled frogs, sat on a speckled log,
Catching some most delicious bugs, yum yum!
One jumped into the pool, where it was nice and cool,
Then there were four green freckled frogs, glug glug!

Four little freckled frogs, sat on a speckled log (etc.)

Three little freckled frogs, sat on a speckled log (etc.)

Two little freckled frogs, sat on a speckled log (etc.)

One little freckled frog sat on a speckled log,
Catching some most delicious bugs, yum yum!
He jumped into the pool, where it was nice and cool,
Then there were no green freckled frogs. Aaah!

ACTIONS
Beaver Scouts jump when the phrase 'jumped into the pool' is sung.

Hey little Beaver

I'm a little Beaver, yes that's me,
We have fun as you can see,
Living in our Colony,
I'm a little Beaver me.

Chorus:
Hey little Beaver, hi little Beaver,
Ho little Beaver, Beaver me,
Hey little Beaver, hi little Beaver,
I'm a little Beaver me.

Chorus:

I'm a little Cub Scout, yes that's me,
We'll have fun as you will see,
With Akela chasing me,
But a little Beaver me.

Chorus:

When I am a Scout, oh yes, that's me,
We'll have fun as you will see,
In the Gang Show there I'll be,
But a little Beaver me.

Chorus:

When I am a Venture Scout that's me,
We'll have fun as you will see,
Chasing Beavers I will be,
But a little Beaver me.

Chorus:

When I am a Scouter, yes that's me
We'll have fun as you will see,
Leading Beavers I will be,
But a little Beaver me.

I'm a little beaver

I'm a little beaver short and stout,
Here's my tail and here's my snout,
When you pull my tail you'll hear me shout,
Hey I'm a beaver, cut that out!

If you're a Beaver and you know it

If you're a Beaver and you know it clap your hands,
If you're a Beaver and you know it clap your hands,
If you're a Beaver and you know and you really want to show it,
If you're a Beaver and you know it clap your hands.

If you're a Beaver and you know it slap your tail *(etc.)*

If you're a Beaver and you know it swim about *(etc.)*

If you're a Beaver and you know it chop down trees *(etc.)*

If you're a Beaver and you know it build a lodge *(etc.)*

If you're a Beaver and you know it shout, 'We are!' *(etc.)*

ACTIONS
Beaver Scouts mime the words as sung. For example, clapping hands, slapping tails, swimming about, chopping a tree, building a lodge.

It's a small, small world

It's a world of laughter, a world of tears,
It's a world of hope and a world of fears,
There's so much that we share,
That it's time we're aware,
It's a small world after all.

Chorus:
It's a small world after all,
It's a small world after all,
It's a small world after all,
It's a small, small world.

There is just one sun and a moon above,
And a smile means friendship to everyone,
Though the oceans are wide,
And the mountains divide,
It's a small world after all.

Land of the silver birch

Land of the silver birch, home of the beaver,
Where the still mighty moose wandered at will.

Chorus:
Blue lake and rocky shore, I will return once more,
Boom diddle li di, boom diddle li di,
Boom diddle li di, boom.

My heart is sick for you, here in the lowlands,
I will return to you, hills of the north.

Chorus:

Swift as a silver fish, canoe of birch bark,
The mighty waterways carry me forth

Chorus:

There where the blue lake lies, I'll set my wigwam,
Close to the water's edge, silent and still.

Chorus:

One, two, three little Beavers

One little, two little, three little Beavers,
Four little, five little, six little Beavers,
Seven little, eight little, nine little Beavers,
Ten little Beaver Scouts.

Pizza Hut

A Pizza Hut, a Pizza Hut,
Kentucky Fried Chicken and a Pizza Hut,
A Pizza Hut, a Pizza Hut,
Kentucky Fried Chicken and a Pizza Hut,
McDonald's, McDonald's,
Kentucky Fried Chicken and a Pizza Hut.
McDonald's, McDonald's,
Kentucky Fried Chicken and a Pizza Hut.

A Burger King, a Burger King,
A greasy cafe and a Burger King,
A Burger King, a Burger King,
A greasy cafe and a Burger King,
A Wimpy, a Wimpy,
A greasy cafe and a Burger King.
A Wimpy, a Wimpy,
A greasy cafe and a Burger King.

A kebab shop, a kebab shop,
A take away and a kebab shop,
A kebab shop, a kebab shop,
A take away and a kebab shop,
A chippy, a chippy,
A take away and a kebab shop.
A chippy, a chippy,
A take away and a kebab shop

A Little Chef, a Little Chef,
A Harvester and a Little Chef,
A Little Chef, a Little Chef,
A Harvester and a Little Chef,
A curry, a curry, a Harvester and a Little Chef.
A curry, a curry, a Harvester and a Little Chef.

Ten brown beavers

Ten brown beavers building up a dam,
Ten brown beavers building up a dam,
And if one brown beaver fell off the dam and swam,
There'd be nine brown beavers building up a dam.

Etc.

The beaver swam over the river

The beaver swam over the river,
The beaver swam over the river,
The beaver swam over the river,
To see what he could see.
And what do you think he saw,
And what do you think he saw,
The other side of the river,
The other side of the river,
The other side of the river,
That's all that he could see.

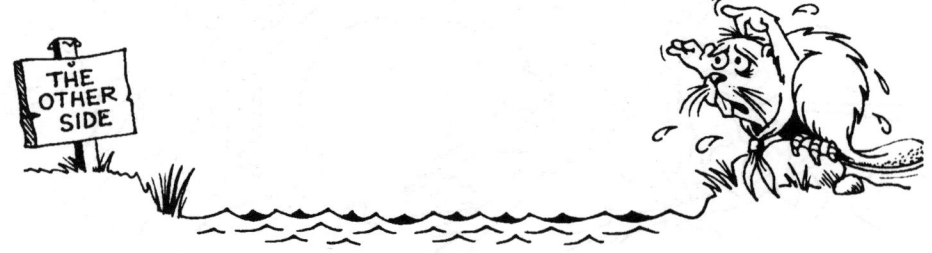

The wee wee song

When I was a wee wee tot,
They took me from my wee wee cot,
Put me on my wee wee pot,
To see if I would wee or not.

When they found that I would not,
They took me from my wee wee pot,
Put me back in my wee wee cot,
And there I wee wee'd quite a lot.

When I was a Beaver Scout in my prime,
I seemed to wee wee all the time,
But now I'm a Leader, old and grey,
I only wee wee twice a day.

Chocolate eclairs

Three chocolate eclairs,
Three chocolate eclairs,
Three chocolate eclairs,
Sitting on a plate,
Gobble, gobble, gobble.

Two chocolate eclairs,
Two chocolate eclairs,
Two chocolate eclairs,
Sitting on a plate,
Gobble, gobble, gobble.

One chocolate eclair,
One chocolate eclair,
One chocolate eclair,
Sitting on a plate,
Gobble, gobble, gobble.

No chocolate eclairs,
No chocolate eclairs,
No chocolate eclairs,
Sitting on a plate,
Blurrrh!

One chocolate eclair *(etc)*.
Blurrrh!

Two chocolate eclairs *(etc)*.
Blurrrh!

Three chocolate eclairs *(etc)*.
Blurrrh!

We are the red men

We are the red men tall and quaint,
In our feathers and war paint.

Pow wow, pow wow,
We're the men of the old dun cow,
All of us are red men,
Feathers in our head men,
Down amongst the dead men,
Ugh! Pow wow, pow wow.

ACTIONS
Beaver Scouts improvise an Indian war dance.

The worm song

Nobody likes me, everybody hates me,
I think I'll go and eat worms,
Long worms, short worms, fat worms, thin worms,
Worms that squiggle and squirm,
Cut their heads off, suck their juice out,
Throw their skins away,
Nobody knows how much I grow on worms three times a day.

Camp fire's burning

Camp fire's burning, camp fire's burning,
Draw nearer, draw nearer,
In the gloaming, in the gloaming,
Come sing and be merry.

(Note:- This can be sung as a round in 4 parts.)

We're all together again

We're all together again, we're here, we're here,
We're all together again, we're here, we're here,
And who knows when we'll be all together again,
Singing we're all together again, we're here, we're here.

Ging gang gooli

Ging gang gooli gooli gooli gooli watcha,
Ging gang goo, ging gang goo,
Ging gang gooli gooli gooli gooli watcha,
Ging gang goo, ging gang goo.
Hayla - hayla shayla - hayla shayla hayla hoo,
Hayla - hayla shayla - hayla shayla hayla hoo,
Shally-wally, shally-wally, shally-wally, shally-wally
Oompah, oompah, oompah.

ACTIONS
The singers are divided into two groups. All sing the song through, then group 1 keeps up the 'Oompah, oompah', whilst group 2 starts again. When they meet at the end, group 1 sings the words and group 2 takes over the 'Oompah, oompah'.

God's love is like a circle

God's love is like a circle,
A circle big and round,
And when you have a circle,
No ending can be found,
And so the love of God,
Goes on eternally,
For ever and for ever,
I know that God loves me.

I know a song that'll get on your nerves

I know a song that'll get on your nerves,
Get on your nerves,
Get on your nerves,
I know a song that'll get on your nerves,
Get, get, get, on your nerves.

I know a song that'll get on your nerves,
Get on your nerves,
Get on your nerves,
I know a song that'll get on your nerves,
Get, get, get, on your nerves.

Kum by yah

Kum by yah, my Lord, kum by yah,
Kum by yah, my Lord, kum by yah,
Kum by yah, my Lord, kum by yah,
O Lord, kum ba yah.

Someone's singing, Lord (etc.)

Someone's laughing, Lord (etc.)

Someone's crying, Lord (etc.)

Come by here, my Lord (etc.)

Old MacDonald

Old MacDonald had a farm, ee-i, ee-i, oh,
And on that farm he had a cow, ee-i, ee-i, oh.

Big cow, little cow, little cow, big cow,
Fat cow, thin cow, thin cow, fat cow,
Old MacDonald had a farm, ee-i-, ee-i, oh.

And on that farm he had a pig, ee-i, ee-i, oh.

Big pig, little pig, little pig, big pig,
Fat pig, thin pig, thin pig, fat pig.
Big cow, little cow, little cow, big cow.
Old MacDonald had a farm, ee-i, ee-i, oh.

And on that farm he had ....
(ask the group for the next animal).

Do your ears hang low?

Do your ears hang low?
Do they wobble to and fro?
Can you tie them in a knot?
Can you tie them in a bow?
Can you toss them over your shoulder
Like a regimental soldier?
Do they wobble in a robble?
Do your ears hang low?

ACTIONS
Actions:
Line 1	Put fingers on ears and mime them curling downwards.
Line 2	Wobble hands to and fro in front of you.
Line 3	Mime tying a knot and pulling it tight.
Line 4	Mime tying a large bow.
Lines 5-6	Toss both hands over one shoulder.
Line 7	As line 1.